Keyboard Runs for the Pop & Jazz Stylist

By Noreen Grey Lienhard

 Complete With Demonstration CD

CD Contents

Swing & Society

Runs: 1 2 3 4 5 8 9 10 13 14
15 16 17 18 19 20 21 22 23
24 25 33 36 38 41 43 44 52

Blues

Runs: 1 3 4 8 12 15 16
17 20 24 25 27 42

Bebop Runs

Runs: 1 5 12 16 18 22 29 30
39 45 53 55 56 61 76 82

Modern Runs

Runs: 1 2 3 4 7 8 9

Etude & Improvisation Using The Runs

TABLE OF CONTENTS

How To Use This Book

Every keyboard player, no matter how experienced, is always on the lookout for a great new run. Jazz musicians copy them, note-by-note, from the recordings of their idols. Blues afficianados flock to see their favorite artists in the hope of bringing one or two authentic-sounding runs home with them. Society-style pianists include them in their published pop arrangements, for students to relish and learn.

Runs bring style and flair to a musical performance. They help define the sound-world of the music being played, and they can impart a professional edge to an otherwise ordinary rendition. People love hearing (or seeing) a pianist run his or her fingers gracefully across the keys; and musicians love the feeling of executing a pattern or embellishment that fits smartly (and sometimes elegantly) into the musical fabric of a song or improvisation.

With all the different performance techniques and genres in music, no single collection of runs can be exhaustive. But this book can help you to build an inventory of runs in a variety of styles, and act as a foundation for developing others on your own.

How should you use these patterns and typical keyboard "riffs" in your playing? There are countless ways. They can be inserted as fills anytime the music offers space for a little added flourish. They can serve as part of your introduction to a tune, or act as a colorful addition to an ending. They can be models for use in improvised solos; pull them out whenever you want a bluesy sound, or a modern one, or when you want to build long, weaving lines in the tradition of jazz greats like Charlie Parker or Bud Powell.

Each of the runs in this book—which is divided into stylistic categories—is presented in several keys. To get the most out of your practice, play them in each of these keys, and then transpose them into a few more on your own; that way you will have them "at your fingertips," no matter what key you may be playing in at a given moment. Try slow practice at first, and then speed the runs up—but only at a comfortable pace. If you want to play something fast, it's important to put enough time into practicing it slowly so that the result is clean, clear and relaxed.

Finally, at the end of the book we have presented a jazz etude on which I created an improvised solo. You'll hear it on the accompanying CD, along with many of the runs, which are played both slowly and at full tempo (the ones that appear on the CD are indicated in the book with a special sign). As you listen to the improvisation, follow along in the book and you'll notice that I've used many of the runs you have practiced—and created some variations on them as well. I've simply inserted these runs over the appropriate chords, with the intention of making a musical "whole"—something that works melodically and that is in keeping with the spirit of the original piece. Studying my spontaneous approach will give you an idea of how to insert your favorite runs into your own improvised solos.

Above all, have patience. The more you play with these runs, the more you will expand your abilities to use them. They are a great tool—and they'll also bring you hours of fun. Happy playing!

The icon  **indicates that a particular run may be heard on the CD.**

Society
&
Swing-Style
Runs

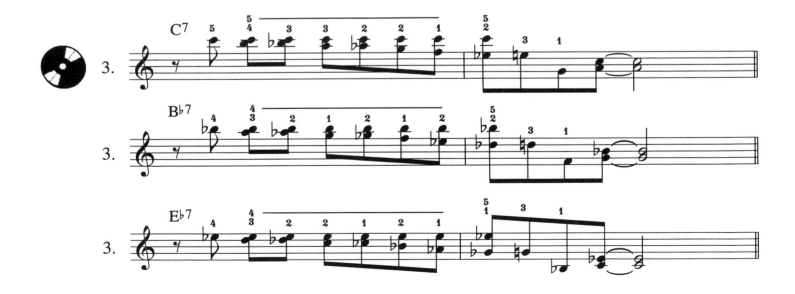

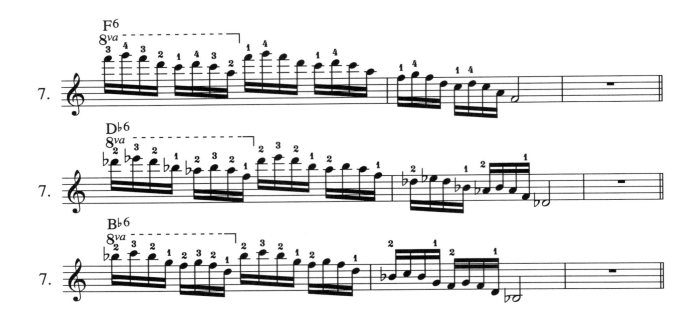

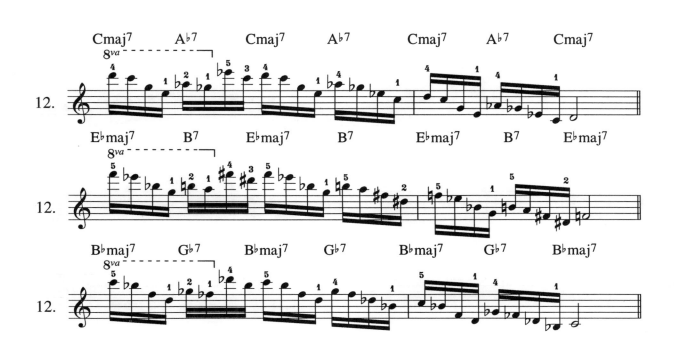

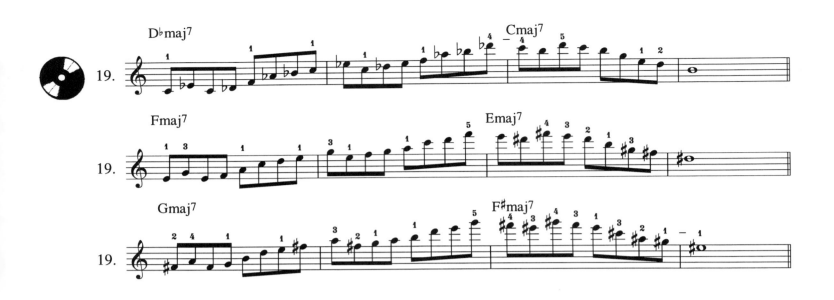

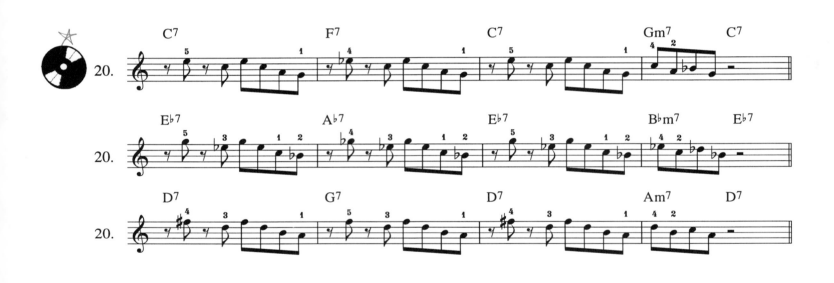

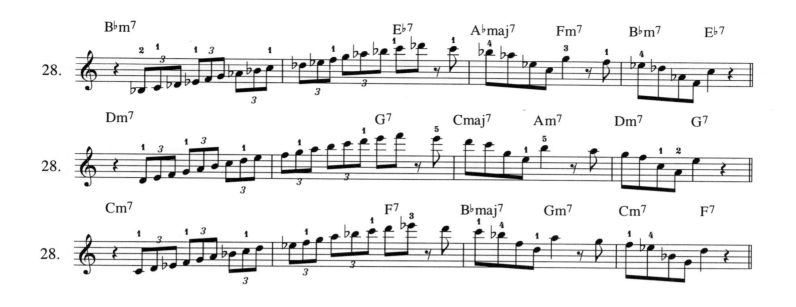

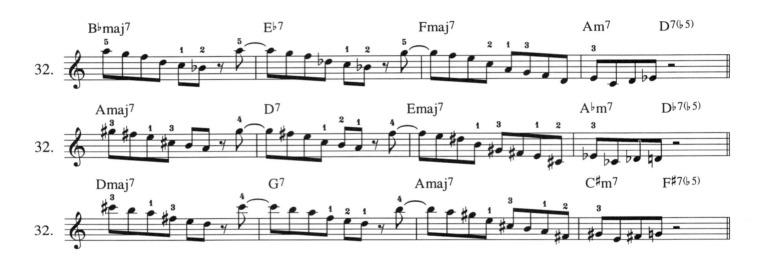

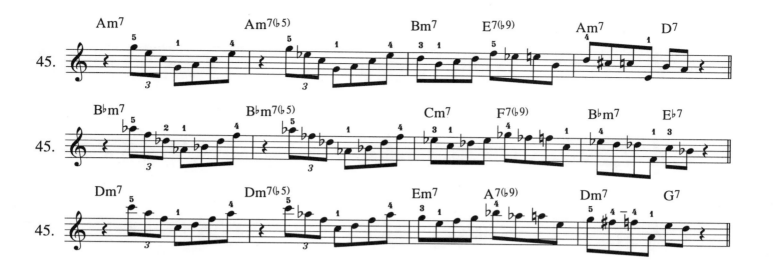

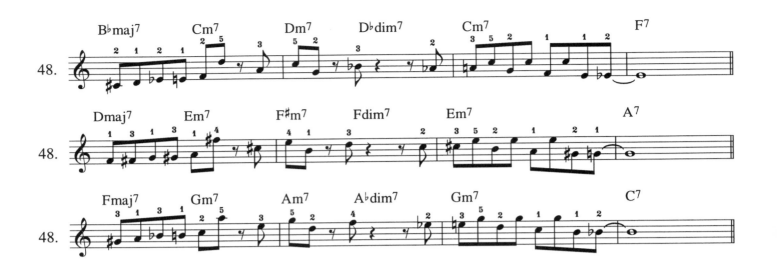

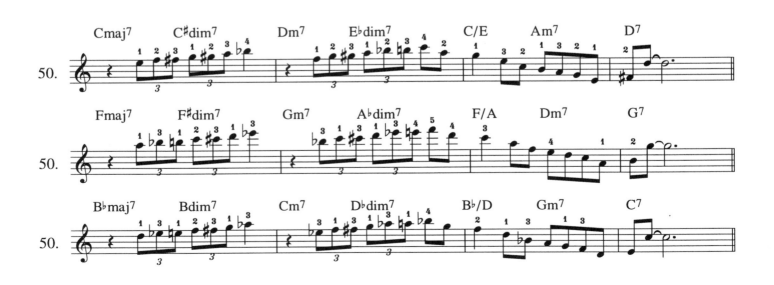

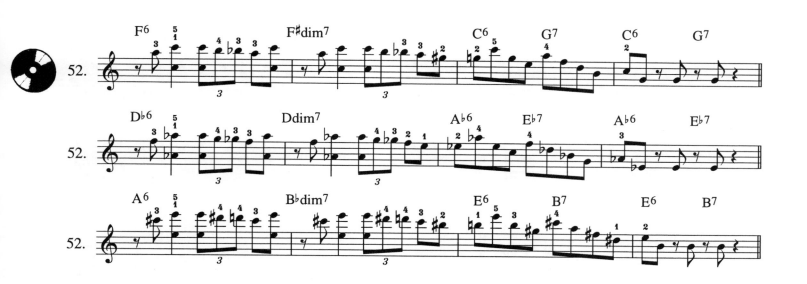

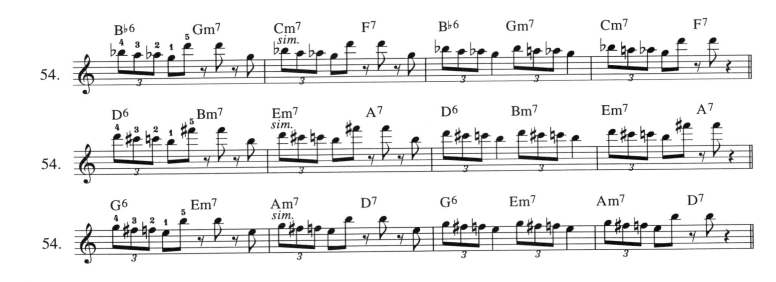

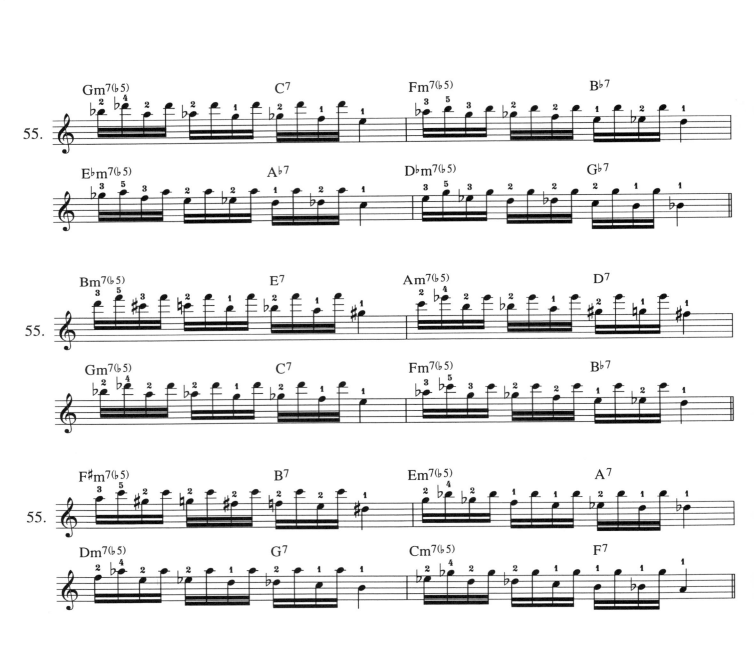

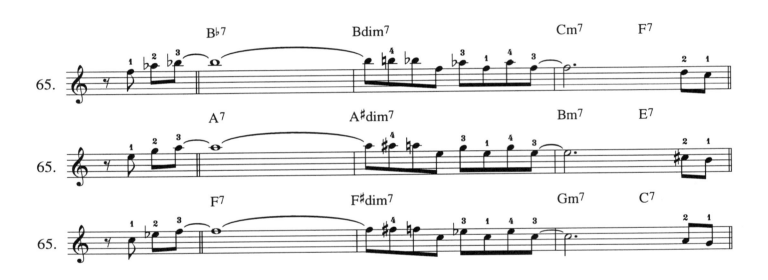

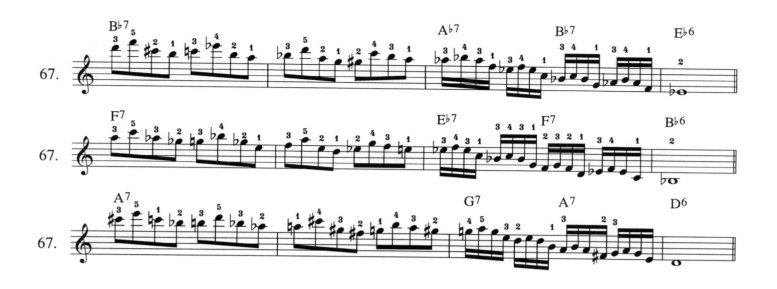

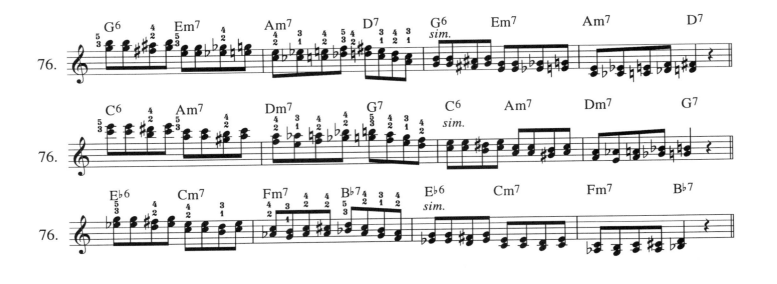

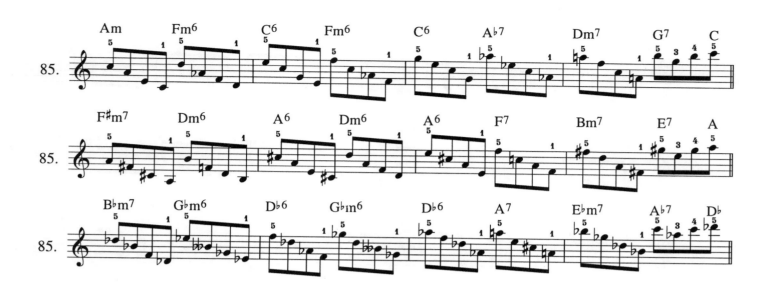

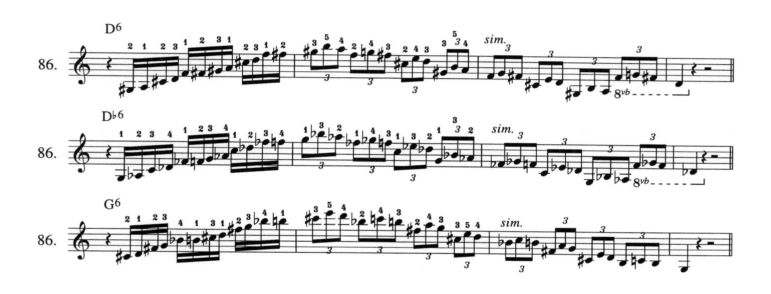

Blues Runs

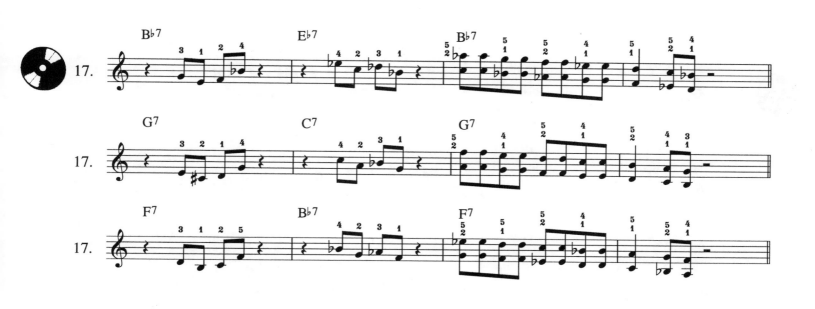

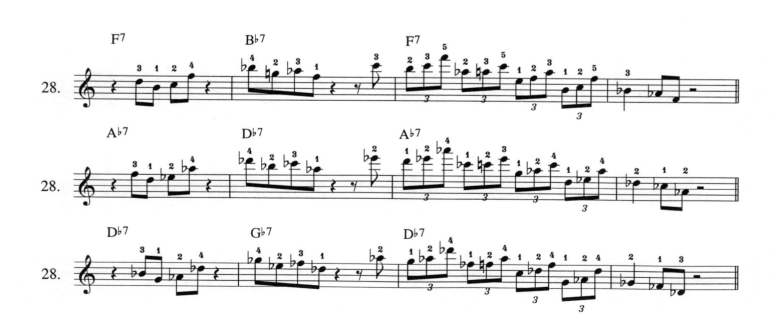

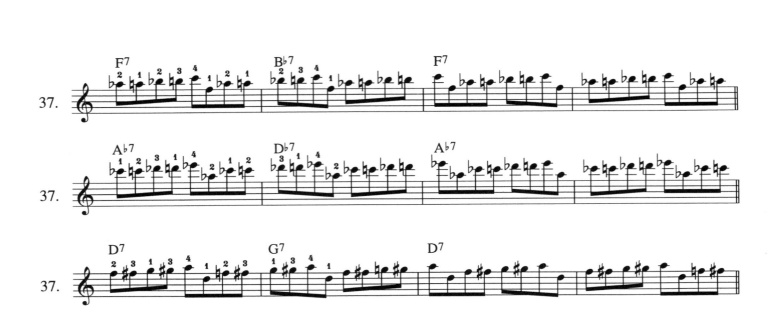

Bebop Runs

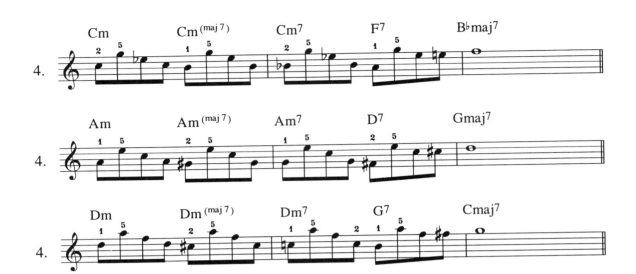

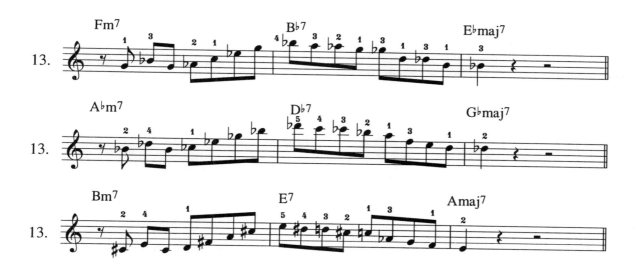

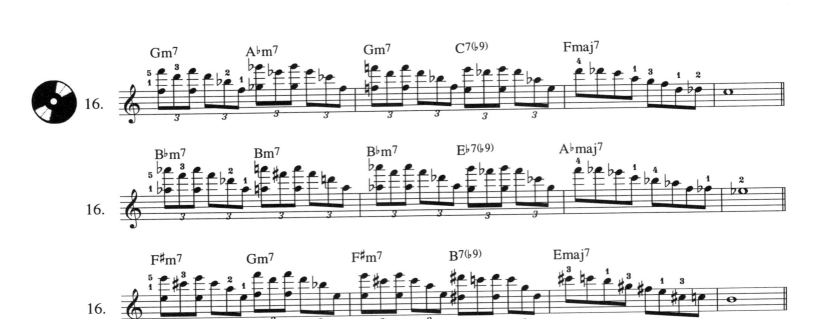

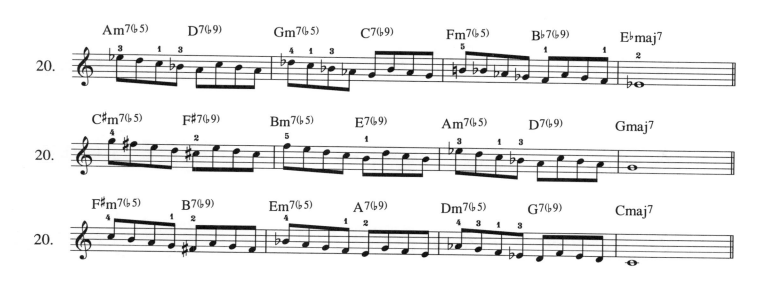

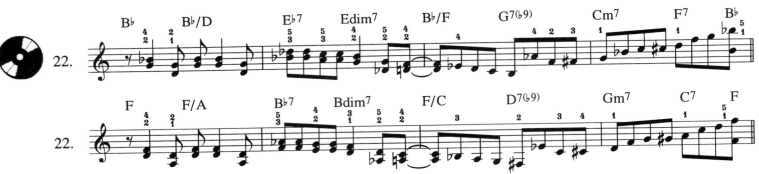

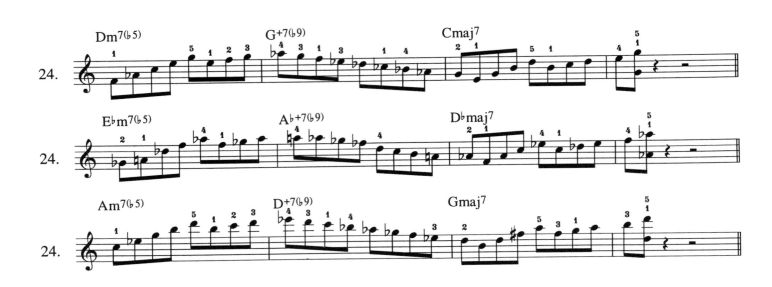

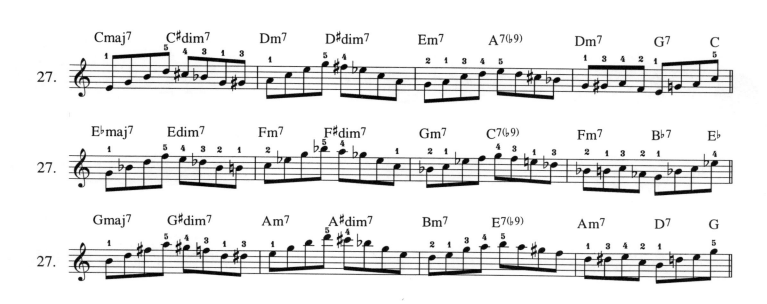

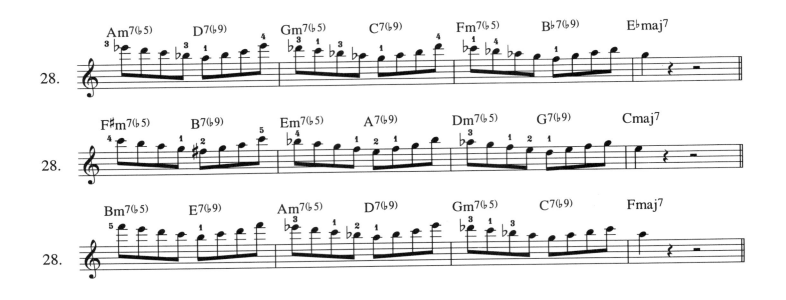

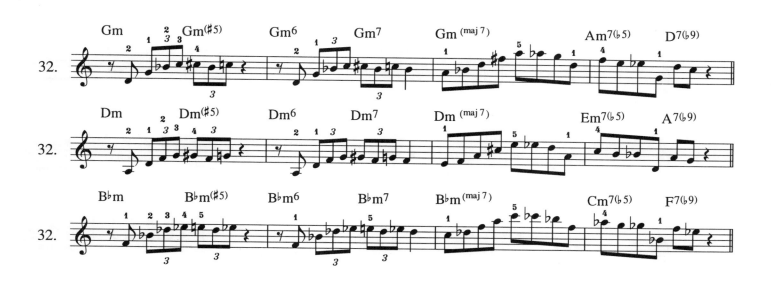

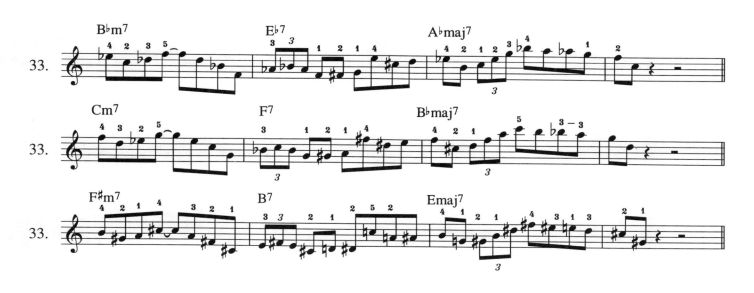

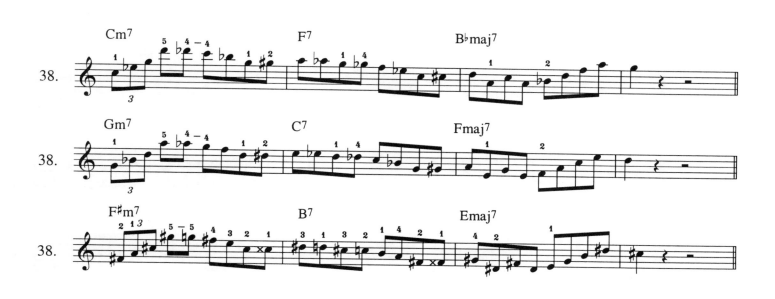

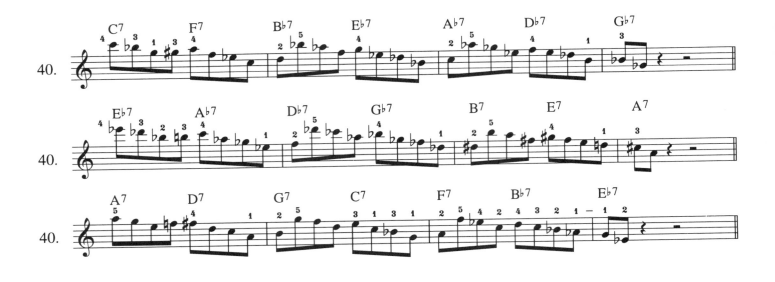

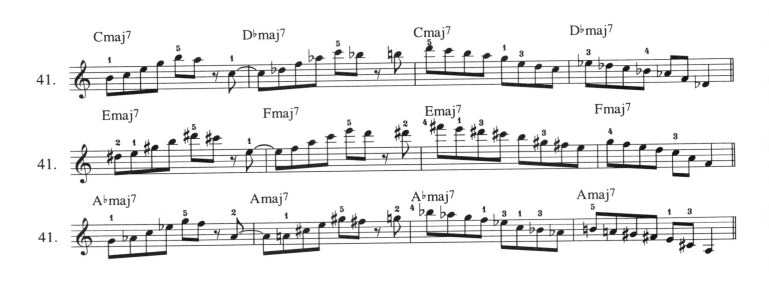

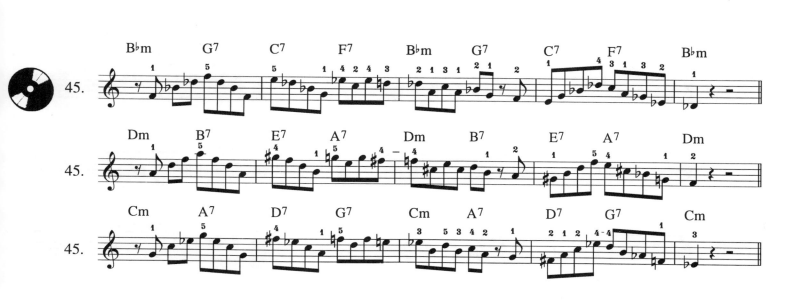

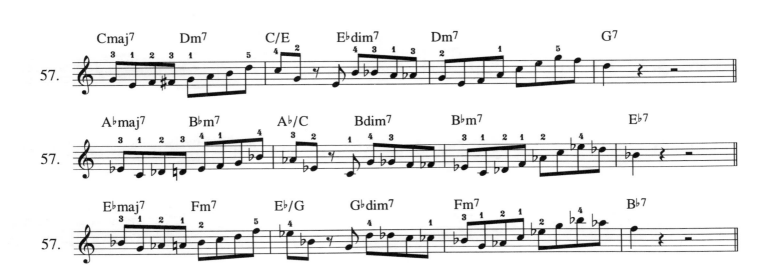

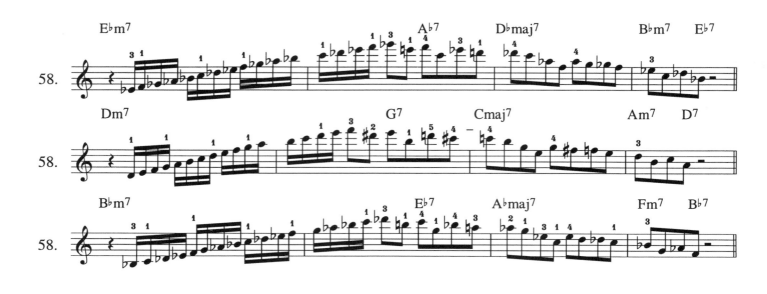

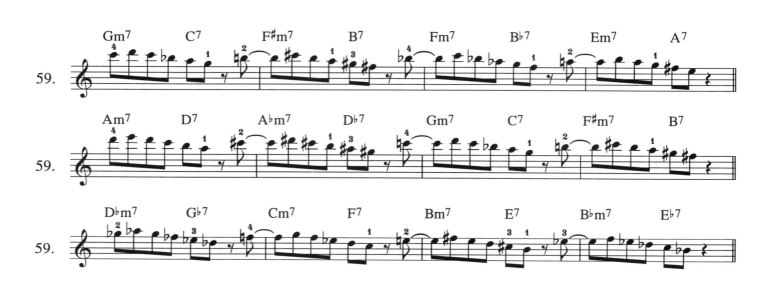

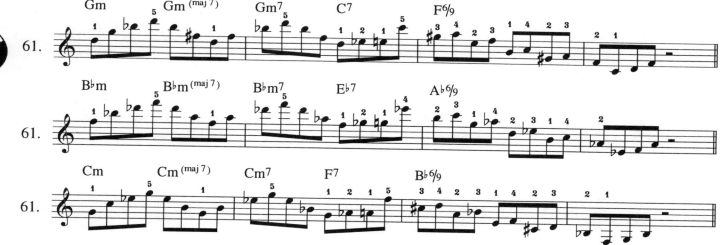

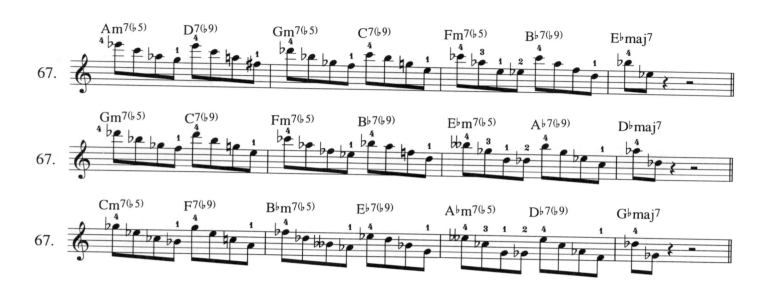

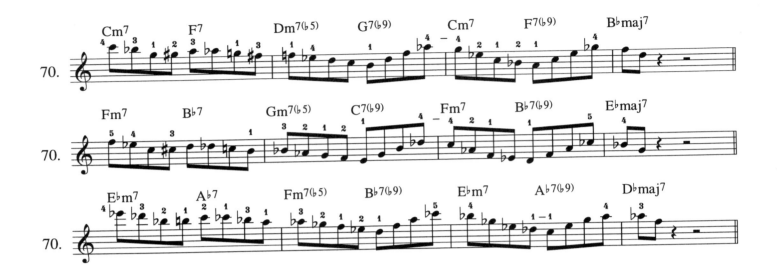

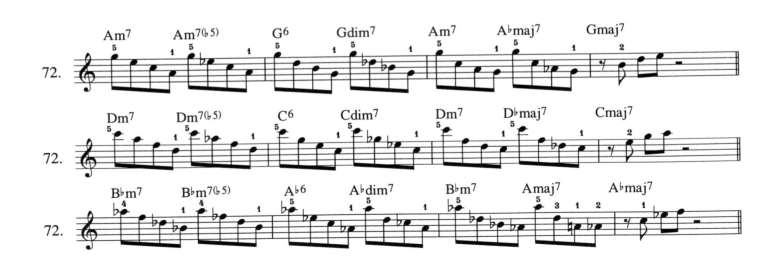

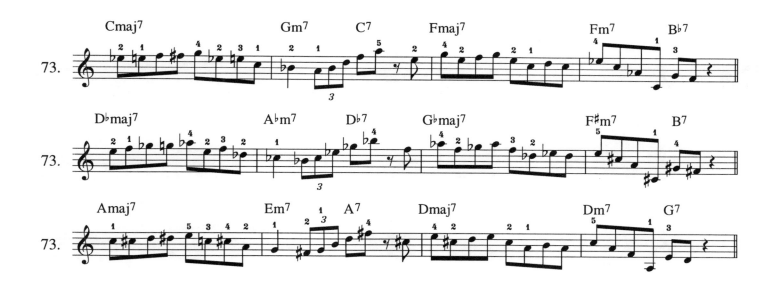

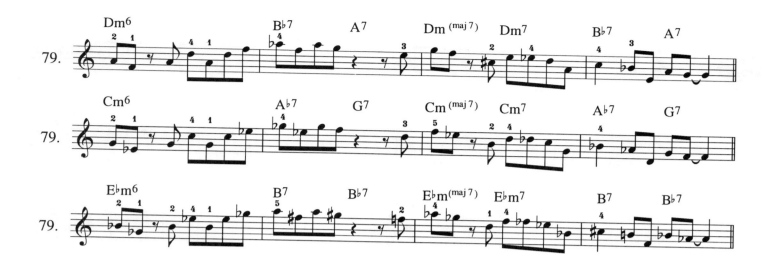

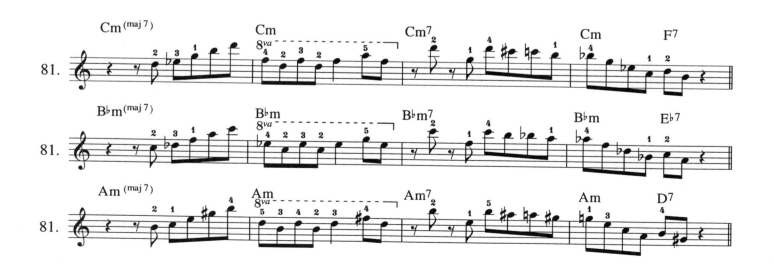

82.

82.

82.

Modern Runs

1.

1.

1.

2.

2.

2.

3.

3.

3.

4.

4.

4.

5.

5.

5.

6.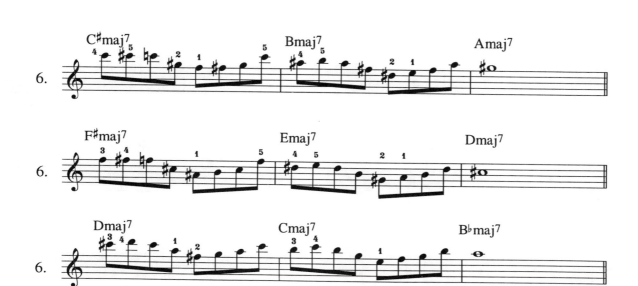

6.

6.

7.

7.

7.

8.

8.

8.

9.

9.

9.

Etude & Improvisation Using The Runs

Etude & Improvisation

Noreen Grey Lienhard

About The Author

Noreen Grey Lienhard has performed with such jazz luminaries as Stan Getz and Joe Morello. She is on the jazz faculty of William Paterson College in Wayne, New Jersey, and has taught at the University of Bridgeport and many other educational institutions. Noreen's other Ekay Music books include *Professional Stylings For The Solo Pianist* and, with Preston Keys, *It's Easy To Be Great*.